T0118502

WIDE EYES CLOSED

WIDE EYES CLOSED

WRITTEN BY
LIBERTY CARRINGTON
COLUMBIA, SOUTH CAROLINA

authorHOUSE®

AuthorHouse™
1663 Liberty Drive
Bloomington, IN 47403
www.authorhouse.com
Phone: 1-800-839-8640

© 2013 by Liberty Carrington. All rights reserved.

No part of this book may be reproduced, stored in a retrieval system, or transmitted by any means without the written permission of the author.

Published by AuthorHouse   12/13/2012

ISBN: 978-1-4772-9389-8 (sc)
ISBN: 978-1-4772-9388-1 (hc)
ISBN: 978-1-4772-9387-4 (e)

Library of Congress Control Number: 2012922212

Any people depicted in stock imagery provided by Thinkstock are models, and such images are being used for illustrative purposes only.
Certain stock imagery © Thinkstock.

This book is printed on acid-free paper.

Because of the dynamic nature of the Internet, any web addresses or links contained in this book may have changed since publication and may no longer be valid. The views expressed in this work are solely those of the author and do not necessarily reflect the views of the publisher, and the publisher hereby disclaims any responsibility for them.

Table Of Contents

Introduction

It has been told to me that I am great beyond measure. Although I have heard this for many years I just could not see because I was plagued by excuses created not only by me but by some of those intimate to me. I did not scribe everyday because I began to fill my mind with garbage and occupy my time with things that were not conclusive to my success. So one day this statement that I have heard a many a time was stated by someone and finally I decided to get off my hind parts and finish my book. I have worked so hard and invested many hours and years to give the people a piece of my mind and a different point of view. If you believe that you are great then never look back and don't let someone or anyone for that matter discourage you and tell you that your goals are unachievable.

You long to be the reflection of me
Though I am imperfect, I am still qualified
With aberrant actions and cogitations
Undamaged I remain accomplished and fulfilled.

Wide Eyes Closed

This book is for the young adults to the baby boomers. Anyone with an interest in poetry, relationships, love, and life in general. This book was written to inspire people to express themselves in other forms versus dealing with the issues in an irrational manor. Many have problems communicating and expressing themselves, so with this art form, I hope to inspire people to form expressions through art and not violence.
Liberty Carrington

Dedication Page

I would like to thank first and farmost My Heavenly Father, Mom, Dad, Genesis, Elija and my husband Antwan. There is one person I didn't mention but without you I would not be here. So with that said thank you Da for watching over me you are truly missed. Many have contributed to this work of art although they may not have known that their situations would have been explained in such a lyrical context. Thanks to those who confided in me and ask me for advice because without you, many of these pieces would not have been possible. Thanks to all of those who listened to me as I VEXED THEM IN THE LATE NIGHT.

Contributors to this Book
Sally San Juan
Willie West
Leslie Porter

Progeny & Sisters

SYNOPSIS

In this chapter, I was in many a mood. It is based upon my family, friends and the beginning stages of serious relationships and why we as people are stereotyped. You will see that I too am an emotional person although the cover portrays a totally different persona. I have a couple of peoms in this chapter dedicated to my ladies and one is in commemoration to a dear friend of mine who has been truly missed. These poems are spoken from my point of view and I hope that you all enjoy my lyricism.

Black

Black, what is black?
What is being black?
Some people who are black can't even answer that,
Because they were taught by a black hole, a mind that is hollow
They might as well be called insane
Because they're not mentally sound
Thinking they could drive on this two lane highway without no eyes
What direction do you think your soul lies?
You're mindless you're not just like the rest
Stand there and stare, as I walk through the gates of glory
You can't even figure out your own blood story
Let me drain it out of you and you shall see a rainbow,
What do you care; you don't even know who made you appear.
You are a mummy without the sheets
What gratifies you, money that's who

But does God give you the mind
To analyze, to decipher all of life
The who, what and why
You don't want to be with 666
But that's how most of us are walking
My years move faster than your steps
I wonder how you rest even though your mouth moves three hundred sixty
words a minute
I still see you standing there
Out of the twenty or a hundred years you've been here
What are you waiting for till the book closes on your soul
Run black runt to the mountain of Zion
Now let my brother Elijah boast on the words of psalm
Praising thee Almighty God
He rides along an eternal black carpet

With the star being black is hard
They tried to cover our past with cement land
But even cement land cracks, spilling the word
Black, black freedom, black beauty, black sex, black man of men black image
of the Lord of host, keep his words' afloat.

Walk with your brother and scream
I am the lion head, my complication is black
From absorbing the ray's from my fore fathers' day
I have full lips, because I have a lot to say
I love you just by looking at you my chocolate queen
Let my seed be planted in your womb for eternity
For I want to stay black
I want my nappy dreads back, so they can lock
Onto the original origin of man, BLACK MAN
ADAM was created out of black mud on the river banks of the Caspian Sea
"BLACK MAN"
MOSES hand was restored to his original color before hand it was as white
as snow "BLACK MAN"
SOLOMON "I am black but comely" "BLACK MAN"
YESUS' feet were like fine bronze as if burnt in a furnace "BLACK MAN"

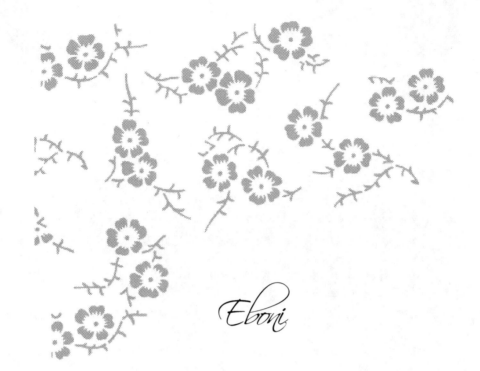

Eboni

I thought of you as my sister
You died and I said babe I'm gonna miss her
I remember all the good times
Sometimes feeling out of minds
Sit and watch the kids run and play
Having discussions about the Bible and pray
When we weren't doing that
We were making a sack
Chillin out sitting on the porch
Light em up and get torched
We would roll up another one
Before the first blunt was done
We would always talk about the guys
Asking each other questions starting with how and why
You use to say my relationship reminded you of a song
At that time you weren't wrong
The guys could easily get us pissed
But we finally got our one wish
We were both engaged to be married
A baby boy was what I carried
Suddenly you got sick
But you were a hustler and never quit
The kids went to live with your mom because you were down
You didn't even want me to come around
I would come to grease your hair
But you weren't really there
Then a couple of months, a couple of strokes
Whatever the illness, this was no joke
You lost feelings on your left side
You losing your life, open my eyes wide
You became terminally ill

I was kept away against my will
Neither of us could see the kids
Because they found out you had AIDS
They had you in the hospital bed ridden
Due to the pregnancy I was forbidden
All day, every day I would pray that you would stay
But I know one day, my girl, my sister would pass away.

2 gb

Even though I just left
My heart has begun to melt
Miss holding you in my arms
Having you slap my palms
Kissing your chubby cheeks
Counting your ten toes on your precious little feet
Mommie misses you dearly
And I pray that your nights are not dreary
I cried on the first flight
Hopefully I won't cry every night
My love for you is unconditional
This separation is very emotional
But we will make it through
Soon I will be back with you

Together

This night I turn and I toss
Thinking of the people I love the most
Hours have passed and still I toss and turn
As if my body is worn
Earlier couldn't keep my eye lids up
Suddenly rhymes over fill my cup
You are my heart
Like they say in the color purple
We will never part
Together we will lie
Together we will pray
Together we create beautiful art
Together the fire will start
Together we use to work
Together we pop the cork
Together we answer the questions
Together we go in the right directions
Together we stand in the rain
Together we endure the pain
Together we sometimes cry
Then we sit and wonder why

Good Man

I sit here in this contemplative state, scratching my head
Because of something's we as women have said
Devoted to finding a man but first find
Blank for you to analyze your mind
Loved by one, stalked and gawked by others
Blind to the reality of our physical lover
Competing with the one who made us complete
Never thought he felt like a piece of meat
Finally you got your good man
Pushing him away with praying hands
Unknowingly we fall then man notices
That he is not the center of our focus
But just a solution to our mind of carnal
Though we preach be more spiritual
Just like some of us hypercritical hypocrites
Therefore resulting in our hearts being ripped
We ask and try them through conformation
Not realizing the adjustments have caused complications
And our lack of recognition on our fancy of flight
Is causing him to act likewise, slight
Always saying we want him to be real
But to our surprise a to real, then our emotions cause us to be reel
Now our good man is once again being pushed away
And soon thereafter maybe a little too late, you got a lot to say
Said sometime before you wouldn't know a good thing if it slapped you in the
face

Silly, looking stupid with your hands on your waist
Didn't consider though he is man experiences hurt
Never . . . until he disappears in spurts
We all know a good man is hard to find
But we have to able to balance him along with our emotional, spiritual and
fleshy mind.

Happily Ever Awaits

Together with you always wanting to be alone
Timing is never right never the same time zones
Life is abrupt our time is limited
All the possibilities are unrestricted
The time will come when we can no longer
And our nucleus will be somber
This love is irresistible
Our hearts have succumbed
Scared because this feels perfect
As if we are soul mates
Moving on with expectations
Announced but still unprepared
In the same vicinity
But still there is vacancy
No room for simple complacency
An emptiness waiting to be fulfilled
Separation causing our hearts to be exposed to agony
Knowing this love can't be replaced
Or implemented by no other
The passion, the romance, the love
Being missing has become excruciating
The heartbeat has been irregular
Feeling as if it is beginning to crack
Something keeps pulling me back
Wanting you in my life forever
Feeling this way, thoughts never

When

You tried to make me see the unseen
Now I finally see what you mean
As I sit to watch others
Realizing you are not just my lover
When you ask of me, I will rise
Just sitting seems to make you angry inside
I wonder what goes on in your mind
Soul searching or day dreaming
Tell me what did you find
Pondering if I am the one
Because it happened to fast and having too much fun
Praying to the Lord show me the light
The light is standing there to your right
Thing I wanted first like money, respect and power
But the Lord has blessed me with a woman shaped like a glass hour
Consistently striving to meet goals
While I'm standing here with my hand out waiting for you to hold
Our life together is passing by
Family and friends asking why
Wanting to build a house together
Can't get through tough times and stormy weather
Promising one day I will be your wife
Not wasting time but needing to get on with life
Maybe we can have kids someday
And get married in the month of May
We fit like hand and glove
Just wanted to let you know that you are my love

Expressions Un-Told

This day I wanted to call
And tell all
That many see you as materialistic
But to me you are uncharacteristic
Took me a while to grasp your demeanor
Out of life you want so much more
I can't seem to get you out of my mind
I am going crazy inside
No one to express these feelings
And not wanting to cause you unnecessary dealings
This day I cannot seem to sleep
Because I didn't say goodnight and I love you my sweet
Willing to give up so many things
So high in love, I feel like I have wings
Laying here staring at the phone
Wondering if you are laying there staring at the moon
Picked up the phone, I want to dial
Something says just wait a little while
Thinking to myself don't cause havoc
Never knew being in love hurt so much
So I lay here waiting patiently
As my heart cries out momentarily
For the love that you always give to me
But my love for you I need you to see
We have put our hearts on the line
Still waiting on the perfect time
This I will send to you
Confessing my undying love for you
Wanting to make that call
And finally tell all.

Moxie Smitten

SYNOPSIS

This chapter is about courageous love. I found myself in love and a few of my associates also. We experience things never imagined, like painful love. As you read these pieces of art, I only hope you can feel the passion, pain, excitement and experience the unknown as I. I hope to bring tears, chills and inspiration because no one is perfect although we continuously strive.

Love Endlessly

You sound o sad today when I called
Told me yesterday that you balled
You say you couldn't get it together
I say babe I know you will pull it together
You had to go to orientation
You exceed all my expectations
I love the fight in you
That's how this love became true
This started out as lust
I said I love you in August
I have seen how much you have grown
The best man I have ever known
I love your strength
My love for you has no length
You are always teaching
And you are continuously reaching
Always striving to supply
And no one can deny
I love how you love our son
Some things are hard to explain
I know I use to cause you pain
I use to just apologize
Cause I could see the pain in your eyes
I promise never to treat you this way
With you forever my love will stay

I love you eternally
I love you unconditionally
I love you physically
I love you mentally
I love you sexually
My love for you has no limit
This is no life without you in it

Wasted Time

The things I do are because I love you
Although I may or may not have plans
All things are subject to change
I avoid friends to spend time
I decline myself to busy, chasing
Is my time being wasted?
The things I do are because I love you
Always wanting to be close
Can't believe I left my heart open
Available to be broken
But hopefully not vulnerable enough to be stolen
My eyes are slowly swelling with tears
For the moment I pray will never arrive
Is my time being wasted?
The things I do are because I love you
Something, really one thing, we love to play and watch
Can't live without the cuddling and conversation
Being romantic, writing you poetry, or simply rubbing your head, back or
chest
Just makes the intimacy and sex an unimaginable additional pleasure
But still, I ask is my time being wasted

Do you enjoy the things I do because I love you?
Things like greasing or scratching your scalp and brushing your hair
Rubbing your back, chest and even your feet
Making smart money and investment decisions
These things are not required or mandatory
I will still love you forever
Even, if my time has been or is it being wasted.

Lest Thy Love Anew; Blonder

Undone; Thy Shall Never Indulge

Again

As fragmented thoughts escape my memory;
Tears began to fall,
For all the years I tried, and sacrificed;
Freely giving my all
In search for a new experience to turn my life around;
I found, that love hurts.
The anticipation of the emotion that I'm addicted to has been greater than
any prescription.
A self-proclaimed addict of affection;
To pass through the process actually coming to know love tainted;
My heart has been blemished.
Resulting in all the opportunities I've missed;
All the individuals I've dismissed
Overwhelmed with possibilities potential beatitude;
I'm not sure I made all the right decisions.
Either from uncertainty or the simple attitude or mind
I predicated decisions on past experiences
They should have been irrelevant
Let them fall behind and left unmentioned
Looking at what lays ahead beyond the shadows

Otherwise I will remain disoriented
Behold a glass mirror reflects self-image, paranoia runs deep
Love is blind to love blindly is a form of insanity
I have converted to become liberated
Improved yet residual traces remain a factor
It is going to take the MAN and me
To relish someone new
Who is also looking to love anew?

IN CASE THE LOVE IS DIFFERENT MISTAKES ARE INVALID I
SHALL NEVER SPOIL MYSELF AGAIN

Hope

Hope deferred, Hope, Hope is all I have
The street sins of the father was cast down upon the son, a weight far too great for young shoulders to bear
The prickly cravings of my mother (a fast lane lover), forced into motherhood and didn't seem to care
He's a product of his environment; no one will hire him,
Hard to inspire him, the efforts are just too tiring'
You see, they . . .
Said I'll never amount to much, said my future wouldn't shine bright
Grew up in a fatherless scene moms' a dope fiend, slangin' rock at 18, two strikes against me I'm just trying to prove them right
Packing at age 22, boss talk crap what's a young man to do, I'll quit when able
In my heart Hope was strong, Hope will tell me when I'm wrong, "quitting won't put "NO" groceries on the table"
You see I . . .
Stormed out the door hurt and confused, going nowhere fast, ego bruised,
Forgot my journey; forgot my God; called up my boys, "what's up with that job?"
Black mask, gloves to be discreet . . . . car pulls up, I hopped in the back set
Mac 11 in my hand, pull off this 211, four brothers, splitting three hundred grand

In a moment of clarity I can see Hope's hand, "Hey, pull over man"
Hope called me back home . . . .
Inspired by Hope, a second chance at life,
Hope's loyalty cuts like a knife
We went places I alone never dared,
Hope held my hand when I was scared,
Hope be stressing me, and testing me,
But Hope, Hope brings out the best in me

Hope gave me the energy to be somebody, Hope prove to me that I was
somebody
For Hope would rather be alone than with . . . . a nobody
You see . . . .
Hope can care less about my street credential
Hope only sees my untapped potential
At home Hope was strong; Hope will tell me when I'm wrong
Hope got me out of that car before it was too late,
Hope will sit at home and wait, "News flash at 8"
All my boys getting strong armed by the cops
Hope was my rescue tonight & many times before telling me think but I must
stop

Giving me strength, courage, and advice
Hope is helping me change my life
Always there giving a helping hand
Wanting and pushing me to be a better man
Hope is always there to scrutinize
But when will I realize
It is time to face reality
Pretending this life I live is justifiably correct
Living life causing Hope tribulation and abuse
Always using my past as an excuse
So what has kept hope from fading?
The time has come, no more procrastinating
I got my life on track thanks to Hope
No more slangin and hustling dope
Most black men have a similar story
But mine is just a memory
I am no longer a statistic
But a man, trying to make a difference
Hope is what carried me and guided me back to life
Hope led me back to God and God made Hope my wife

Dejected

Being without you has me dejected
Vitriol and adroit yet I remain pious
I parried but undoubtedly it was kismet
Lacking myopia and range . . . .
Somehow I remain stable enough to walk and talk
Neither the less falling into an abyss of emotion pity
Have I fallen alone or will I be accompanied
Engulfed and or hitting rock bottom leading us, you, me or we from one
entity to two or three
Should that matter as we have pursued our happiness, ended the cloak and
dagger to be lonely no longer as one
Enraged with love as we embark on this forsaken endeavor
Warmhearted always, hearts are never derelict for we have fulfilled,
regardless the arduous attempts to become one

Revoked

For sometime I was pursuing this chick
She looks good enough to lick
One day she was approachable
And finally I was noticeable
I took her snorkeling on Sunday
I bought her a hot fudge sundae
And the opportunity to lick aroused
Thought of buying her a rose
She was late to arrive
Wonder how it feels for her to ride
I said let's get something to drink
Happening so fast no time to think
I never thought I would have this chance
Didn't have time to romance
Now I'm making figure eights
Thinking this is my soul mate
So good I want to release inside
Couldn't believe she had my mind
Wanted her more than a one night partner
Home is the one I met at the alter
Will you be my girlfriend?
No responses until the end
Wife and girlfriend on my hands
Now I am no longer superman
Ole girl is always inspirational
And always motivational
Wifey is always irritating
And accusing me of cheating
Tranquility is now the situation
Finally no more agitation
Doing things I'd rather not mention

I can't believe their renditions
Ole girl giving me sexual healing
Wifey giving me constant kneeling
One is an undercover freak
Got me biting on the sheets
The other is always a lady
And wants to have my baby
Both ladies are requiring more attention
I can sense cruel intentions
Wife is answering my phone
Girlfriend scratching my chrome
My wife is all in my face
Girlfriend doesn't know her place
So I try to stay away
Shit piles on every day
This is a fucked up position
Both women are missing

Drama

Our lives have been created into a melodrama
Living life the way we have created melodrama
To us so unnecessary but yet surreal
To them we have been excessive
Them to us, disloyal but somehow justified
But we have continued to love, them
Without loving ourselves and diminishing our love for each other
Yearning to be the queen of all women
As you my king and man of men
Though the situations are disrespectful, there is happiness
Happiness well deserved, worth crying
Morality is compromised, but virtuous upon us

Notions

You have given me an alternate view
None to compare, not even a few
I realized that we are connected
These feelings I do not want redirected
Through many more ways than we may know
For my face and eyes by no means may show
Each and every one of the smiles you continuously leave on my face
No one can ever erase
I attempt to satisfy you in every way
Mentally, physically and sexually every day
May we dine and savor the flavor of filet mignon
While we toast with 2004 Cabernet Sauvignon
Afterwards we will share a dance
Each other we will endlessly romance
I am yearning to be with you every minute
I cannot envision my life without you in it
It is difficult to imagine my life
Not being your wife

Fathom

In a place so unfamiliar and unfair
In love with someone else continuously withholding tears
Thinking if I had made different decisions previously
Would I be in this state of unconsciousness?
Or the temporary state of mind that we all know as happiness.
Lying in the bed holding a pillow; lonely.
Wanting you to hold me, breathe on my neck
Hands on my waistline, awaken dripped in sweat
Only to realize that this is my consciousness
Not a dream of what, whom, or where I desire
I apologize, l love, but to love, a liar.
You love, I complaint your faults, faultless
Not by far but capable of recognizing my imperfections
Therefore there are warning signs prior to the altercation
But so inattentive and it doesn't even matter
Then I take my best approach
And here you are stuck because the lights are on, I scattered roach
Fighting useless right now and for some time now I could not and still can't
see the happily ever after.

Restless

The excitement and passion we shared has me restless
Only to find that you are well rested without me
You say that you're in love
And yes it's evident through obvious abandonment
So hurt by the lack of consideration
Is finally felt and the feeling is likewise
Seems like racing time nothing like wine
Together when we come wishing we could press rewind
But only existing in our imagination looking abroad
For in reality there is no fast forward
Sadden by the reality of my life and yours
Sitting around thinking, twiddling thumbs bored
Missing the excitement and passion, restless
Ultimately matched unknown outcome priceless
Stressed from this mess so confused
Feeling lost, yet loved, and some way just can't figure it but misused
Or will the restlessness be the execution
Because waiting for your restitution
Has me wondering if I am the one executing
Myself and others with this heart of steel no longer percolating
With love but purely excitement and passion that is
Until someone writes my autobiography thesis

Trudging Vitiation

SYNOPSIS

I wrote these poems when I was in a state of disarray. I could not wrap my mind around why men treat women the way they do and vice versa; corrupt the good one and their adoration for the scrub is sincere. Therefore these runes are filled with desires unfulfilled, in the search of happiness. Still I wonder, what is happiness? From me to you it is different amongst all of us, none defined the same. Searching to find is useless for you have become the prey. Process, reminisce and excogitate your hustle.

King Of Queens

You say I am for life
Used to come, kiss, and fill me
No longer needing to talk
Finally got your way
There is no need for the one
Putting so many things on the line
Can't even afford to bluff
Can't decide who is full of
Though you are the king
You say that I am joy
But you seem to be elated
You use to miss
But I am desolate
Always wanted to be Superman
Beseeching my wishes and desires
Making inquires about my dreams and goals
Wanted my mind, body and soul
Asserting you want only the best
All you solicited you got, but it's blazing
With out the king to extinguish

Creatures

Men are emotional creatures only exposed as they pull back their prepuce.
Got women losing their minds, disobeying their own rules, looking back
what's the use?
Trying to analyze in your mind why he did the things he did to contaminate
your mentality
But when you open your eyes no longer blinded you will see as he reminisces
u have become his fatality.
Using you for sex and money
Now he out there whining about I'm broke and your pussy the best; hungry
Then he got the nerve to say it's over because you're emotional
But it's cool with you because you realize that not only is he unstable but lonely
Nigga you a muthafucking phony, full of dreams with no means of
accomplishments
Looks good, cockiness a perk, unconventional a plus, equals to me potential
Now time has passed and reality has set in and all that potential is one
dimensional
Assay all the special occasions and just moments wanted to be shared missed
With the excuse "I gotta work" unknown until the money you dismissed
And this sorry excuse of he who calls himself a man took all you gave
Didn't even consider all the times you laid, paid, didn't get spade because you
didn't want him sleeping with the maid
And the thanks you get from this unappreciative, self-centered creature
Is pain unable to be explained numb; teacher
Not only to fall as leaves to their feet because his talk was sweet, good meat,
head flawless, body and he made me feel like no other
Here to speak that you have not experienced every brother,
Gentlemen patient to be your lover
Not all so listen, adhere to the warning signs
And don't believe all the lies, shoo flies.
Eliminate to elevate above those trying to mollify
The words motivating elation, Fly.

Concoction

Lately we have appeared to be lonely
No one to express the stress, because
They have no way of relating or advocating
Claiming they want to listen and provide advice
Just gathering information to cause impediments
Not realizing the trust bestowed upon them
Releasing secrecy with whom they lay
Even though they have diminished your hardships
Our tribulations are not theirs to create lies
Implicating that you are my
Brother, sister, friend, boy or girl
"I love you like" and only have your best interest
It appears that our reliance is being divulged
Instead of asking we, the one
You would rather ask others
Who think they know, but are oblivious?
Here and now the truth is revealed
That the one who exclaimed "I love you like"
A brother, sister, friend, boy or girl
Created this jaded concoction
That caused us to be lonely.

Pisstivity

You act like such an ass
Then you wonder why I smoke all the grass
It's like you're wearing a mask
And I'm the one exposed to your nuclear gas
I am suppose to be your wife
The one whom you will spend the rest of your life
But it doesn't see that way cause your words cut like a knife
You make cruel jokes and think they are funny
Always starting arguments always about money
Sometimes I feel like I'm not your honey
You look at me as if in disgust
Not with love and lust
Always talking shit
Knowing how much I dislike it
I respect that you are older
But everything I do receives the cold shoulder
Nothing I do is enough
Your attitude makes things rough
Nothing I say seems to matter
Like you repeating yourself is going to make things better
Lately you have been an asshole
Stuck to my face like a mole
You love getting me pissed
Oh how I wish I had one wish
That you would be the man I fell in love with
Yes I expect things to change
Because I know they can't stay the same
Which is obvious because I changed my name?
Baby I love you without a doubt
I ask that you just chill out
You acting like you do get on my nerves

Feels like I'm bending around steep curves
You say you love me and you care
But that's not what I feel from your stare
I try to give you everything you want
In the end it turns out that you don't
If things don't go your way
For me hell is on the way
I got to deal with your mouth
All good things turn south
If things don't go exactly as planned
Walk around here like you the man
No positive outlook on anything
Always blaming me for everything
It's like you love me with limitations
Sorry I don't meet all your expectations

Plague

You have polluted my environment
A disease with no cure
Cautious of what I say and do
I may become infected or my words are misconstrued
A snake disguised as a lizard
This can't possibly be poisonous
Not only but it is contagious, transmittable, and fatal
Affecting my good-nature with your maliciousness
The devil's advocate in an angel's cloak
Not to deify myself but I despise
Fake individuals with no individuality
Created by experimentations
Successful but flaws are
Seeing yet never seen
Successful yet to be unseen
Protected yet never known to its protector
Seeing finally to see
You have become my plague
Known for being a fatal disease
But your fixation with me
So addicted you found my stash
Absentminded by my drug
Has you being oblique never to be relaxed
Overwrought, overdosed on the supply
Ever so gently I overcome
I have found your cure
Insanity, attacking me habitually
Plagued

C.I.D. (Crazy, Insane, Derange)

I hate to see me in this pain
That I am not only enduring
Everyone is watching and feel I am to blame
Faking innocence and sane
But the craziness everyone seems to be ignoring
Pretending to be hurt, telling lies with fake cries
How would it feel if I endangered your life?
Tried to ruin your life plan
But I am the man
Out here falsifying claiming you love me
I love you until I hate you
Run away trying to avoid
You, with the constant bullshit
I have given up, so tired, this is redundant
Not a quitter, quite persistent; a fighter
You know my past, killing my present, and planning my future
Because you have become an un-stable creature
Crazy, insane, deranged!!!
I will play your retarded game
Although this shit is lame
Always wanting to be in the spot light, this isn't fame
These are some of the reason you can no longer be my dame.

Sinister Miss

Is it that you are insecure?
Or, are you jealous?
That I am sexier, more intelligent
Cheerful, poetic, overflowing with aspirations
That makes me a revelation
I don't give the impression of a bitch
Always mean-mugging, never smiling
Like the devil is always whipping your back side
So caught up in my life
Can't be content with yours
Worried that I am his friend
And maybe, just maybe he wants to philander with me
Because you, are not me
I am friendly but you
You who is not my friend is a friendless shark
I am trying not to scarify your name
Because you are capable of seppuku
To me you are C.I.D. but shenanigan fits you well
You pretend to be schism and sybarite
It is apparent to me that you are sluggard
Opening up your sluice
Hankering me to stucco
My presence to your relationship makes you saturnine
Most females are sagacious
Your sagaciousness is stultified
This leads to daily set-tos
You are a salacious, schlemiel, scamp
Your scabbing, has become sardonic
It is senescent, and your sage waits
This is me to you, friend to friendless
Satire but not scurrilous

Sinister Miss 2

Is it that you are insecure?
Or, are you jealous?
That I am sexier, more intelligent
Cheerful, poetic, overflowing with aspirations
That makes me a revelation
I don't give the impression of a bitch
Always mean-mugging, never smiling
Like the devil is always whipping your back side
So caught up in my life
Can't be content with yours
Worried that I am his friend
And maybe, just maybe he wants to philander with me
Because you, are not me
I am friendly but you
You who is not my friend is a friendless shark
I am trying not to scarify your name
Because you are capable of suicide by disembowelment
To me you are crazy, insane, and deranged but shifty with questionable
behavior fits you well
You pretend to be in a religious body and devoted to pleasure and luxury
It is apparent to me that you are lazy
Opening up your mouth
Wanting me to close

My presence to your relationship makes you depressed
Most females have keen perception
Your perception is useless
This leads to daily angry conflicts
You are an indecent, stupid, mischievous person
Your hard work has become sarcastic
It is growing old, and your judgment waits
This is me to you, friend to friendless
Attacking with words but not using abusive language.

Hatin Won't Help

You feel the way I did you was a shame
Now you fabricating story to put salt in my game
Acting like I promised you infinity
Emailing my Girl "woman to woman" but won't reveal identity
Hoping that you've offended me (I know you fittna be)
Disgruntle cause I dissed you when u was feeling me
You hoes be killing me
Trying to pretend like I ain't kept it 100
Singing the same sad song bitch it's getting redundant
(Girl nigga's ain't shit) at 36 years old the game should have been cleverer
Blaming me for problems take a look in the mirror
Glorifying your younger years through your daughter and her peers
I should've known that before I flew back
I only fucked you in the first place to give Stella her groove back
Bitch move back
No phone calls, text messages, no more emails,
My sex game left you breathless now you are waiting to exhale
Faking sophistication with your quick weave and fake nails
Check your position you doing hair in your kitchen
Ain't been to school and got no license ole fake ass beautician
Shawty listen tell me what I did again
To have a grown ass women acting like a kid again
And mean that in worst way
How you expect to be my girl when I fucked you on the first day
When I met you at the club you was all in my face pop lock and drop it
I didn't show you no love now you all on my space cock blocking bopping
Shawty stop it you making a fool of yourself
I'm a Mack from way back hating just won't help

Cry

I don't want to go, I want to stay
Funny me feeling this way
Every day I stare in their eyes
Continuously withholding my cries
Trying to remain strong
But in my heart this is wrong
Working a job I have to defend
When aching hearts are yet to mend
Afraid, yes I am of death
God, please give me the strength
Praying for so much ore
Always wondering what's in store
With this job you never know
Family asking how long is you doing this for
Causing my family to split
I wish I could quit
Shaking my head every time I see that man
Asking myself how long will he be the man
Only thinking of his success
Destroying our country and others just making a mess
Killing our love ones, family and friends
Just so he can make ends
Destroying peoples American dream
Chilling while your country goes up in flames
Let's open our eyes and we will find
The man in control of these criminal minds
Killing off innocent souls, bodies and minds
Adultery OR endangering your country and murder; which is worst?

Which crime would you punish first?
I don't know why some people love you so much
In my opinion you suck
What happen to strength, courage, and wisdom?
We all knew you were a little dumb
But we had no idea your brain went numb
Slowly but surely we dig up roots
I think it's time we give him the boot
We all make mistakes
I pray that we all learn from the mistakes that we make.

Concupiscent Prose

SYNOPSIS

This is a very short explicit chapter. Only a few poems to make your body tingle, sweat and those private areas begin to throb. Words that will make you want to explore you body as well as that of your signifcant other, lover, or whatever you choose to call that person of whom you are intimate with at any given time. Allow me the opportunity to take you to a place; your temperature is rising, chills on your spine, and a burning passion is in your eyes.

Awaken Suddenly

Awaken suddenly, as thoughts of you cross my mind
Shivering from the chills running up my spine
Looking, I have no idea
Thinking things not to be exposed to the media
Thoughts I said should remain subliminal
Nothing on top or the bottom only wanting to be in the middle
Wanting me to sit on your face
While past lovers memories are being erased
You are holding on to my waist
Awaiting the release of my sweet taste
And both my legs have begun to tremble and shake
Wondering what will come of this lovely love we make

In The Face Part 1

Our clothes we drop to the floor
As soon as we walk through the door
Discovering each other's body without a touch
Wanting each other so much
I spread whip cream over your stomach muscles
You dribble chocolate over my nipples
As you softly kiss my neck
I feel myself getting wet
I nibble on your ear
I rub my fingers through your ceasar
Aroused I think we are there
The chocolate you begin to lick
As I slowly caress your dick
From the nipples, down to the clitoris
My eyes roll back whispering I love this
I reach for something out of the clothes bunch
As you eat me like crunch and munch
Trying to find something to cover my face
As my orgasm comes down I am sure you can taste
Now that you are done
It's my turn to give you one

In The Face Part 2

Give me a second I gotta get my ring
Once I have it I can do my thing
Slowly I drop to my knees
The closer I get the harder you breathe
I begin to lick your thigh
Your dick begins to rise
Your dick I decide to grab
And give you the best head you have ever had
I begin to twirl my tongue around the tip
I watch as you bite your lips
I place an ice cube in my mouth and it creates chill bumps
As I suck I taste the pre-cum
I begin to deep throat and stroke
And suddenly I begin to choke
Your hips start to move
Now I'm in my grove
I go up and down
Twirl my tongue all around
I ease from bottom to top and then I tickle
I feel you begin to wiggle
I hum on your balls
Can't wait for you to be in my walls
Continuously I stroke and deep throat, increasing the pace
Your warm cream waste all over my face

Transcending The Limits Of Thought

SYNOPSIS

This is the final chapter and all these poems are based upon self improvement, motivation, forgiveness and recognition; of who you are, where you intend to be as you progress and overcome obstacles. Many may say that you are snobbish and maverick because you prefer to continuously strive for what you believe to be utopia. Be it your relationship with God, intimate partner or the part of you that is unbecoming in your eyes or societies for that matter. I only hope my words goad you or someone with whom you associate yourself with to continue, for this life is just beginning, we have not finish living for there is so much more within that is undiscovered.

Defeated

This feels like the lowest point
Irritation is elevated, lost, direction unknown
Crying unlimited, no one to fall upon
Annoyed by most but not all
I have fallen
Sinning, praying for forgiveness
I'd rather be, than faking my saintliness
Waiting for my calling but I have not
Or am I oblivious, or is it subliminal?
I have fallen
Unprepared, for the unexpected
Past exceptional, future arbitrary, present shattered
Nevertheless, I have been reduced
Mind, Body and Soul appear to be collapsed
But I will not be defeated
If thou, Lord, should mark iniquities, O Lord, who shall stand?
But there is forgiveness with thee, that thy may be feared.

Dreaming

We have struggled
But how much more can we withstand
It has been stated that words hurt
More than sticks and stones
Spit to my face and water that chills to the bone
We have proven that we can endure
We have had many a dreams
Some of our dreams are not as big as others
Dreams of being poets, writers, philosophers
Educators, doctors, lawyers but many dreams
Have been suppressed by those like us,
Friends, sisters, brothers, lovers' even mothers and fathers

One dream that we are witnesses to today
Is that dream of Dr. King?
And most of all, the dream of Barack Obama
The dream that many of us thought we would never see
But with us being the result of a dream,
Desire, realize, embody, ambition and motivate dreams
Although we may fail at some of our endeavors
Never give up because your journey is not over
"Nothing will work unless you do."
We must always pursue happiness
"We may encounter many defeats but we must not be defeated."
To fail at is not that we are failures but we attempted to change
Society is not prepared for change,
Therefore we who those like us consider failures are not
But we are achievers in search of our blessings
Through all that we have endured
All of the dreams that we have dreamt
Journeys and endeavors that have failed
We still have more to overcome
But yet still we will survive.

Forgiveness

Sitting here twisting my fingertips
Waiting at this very moment to kiss your succulent lips
Acting as if you don't want to visit
Though always crying it is me you miss
Apologies not accepted just heard
Because lies have been compiled
And mistakes are becoming the norm
Wanting so much for you to trust me again
But betrayal prolongs the forgiveness
Nothing can correct the wrongs I have made, nothing
But I refused to be reduced while; I am in the phase of transformation

Battle Within

When you're so used to leaning on someone you forget how to stand alone.
Yet you proclaim to be one who is independent.
And now you're nursing feelings of abandonment.
No longer being constrained but still.
Bound by emotions and restricted with fear.
Mind is traveling, and your body is procrastinating.
On a rollercoaster ride of life with no start or finish.
Lost in thought, feeling demoralized, coveting consummation.
On the verge of swallowing pride and abandoning morals, longing just to try
Escaping the mind-numbing reality but questioning your intentions ill or able-bodied
Yearning to be engulfed in you, mentally, physically, emotionally, and spiritually
Ascertaining who you are, running away is not mandated.
Still trying not to emotionally dwindle holding on to you.
Realizing following one course until successful, is rapture
Reminiscing on our beginning; not wanting to imagine the end.
Longing to be back in the middle of what was neither old nor new.

Life

Constantly questioning yourself, why?
Why am I working just to get by?
Someone at work gets under your skin
Heated like a balloon, all I need is a pin.
Doing all the work with no recognition
Supervisors act like they don't see
Can't see and won't see your ambition
Some living the life of what they see as a thug
Making a living selling folks a drug
Young ladies having multiple abortions
But still lacking what we call an education
Grown women having children just to get a check
House, car and children still a wreck
Raising the prices; Prices such as taxes and gases.
Soon we will all walk around with oxygen masks
Quick to give others the money
We the people can't get a jar of honey
Struggling to make friendships and relationships prevail
When in reality those you fight the hardest for will fail
Friends so long almost like my sister or brother
Went to college grew up and became the other
You know; her, him and then the other
Hurts so bad you feel a sharp pain in your heart
Then, realize we grow up and somehow we grow apart
To those who have businesses, I wish you success
Congrats to those who get their degrees.
Getting a job in your major is no breeze
Remember we made fun of those who took up a trade; we called them
knuckleheads
Look at them knuckleheads making all the bread
Single parents of all genders, salutes to all of you

Your child or children will one day render
Apologies if I missed you, God bless and to Him remain true
Striving to make it tomorrow
Though the world is filled with much sorrow
Filled with strife, but this is life

Self Shit

Lately everyone wants to keep it one hundred
But no one tells all they did
Nigga's lying on they dicks and how many chicks
Broads perpetrating straight knowing they gettin licked
Use to be DL but your actions TELL, TELL
Though your sexuality, you hid well
Exposed now you running away like Kanye
And those one hundred saying yeah
Now you claiming they selfish
Nah just full of self shit
Not fully indulged in yourself
For you are as frail as breathe
Haters on you're back weighing you down
Make ASSumptions, ASS no frown
Sweat explain your judgment
Never mind it doesn't matter just cruel intent
Just like those involved in abomination
But yet this is "The Great Nation", fakin
Tearing you down make you dependent
Still can't see how you proclaim I N dependent
Now you claiming they selfish
Nah just full of self shit
Not fully indulged in yourself

For you are as frail as breathe
Walk in the building IDLE . . . co-workers, just my luck
Yet they make more sometimes less. I know, WTF
Talking hella shit about tax cuts, no raise or bonus
Fighting within ourselves for our lack of focus
But who gets recognition for the work I've done
That lazy motherfucker concocting another one
Running off at the mouth creating a body of lies
For why, may I ask is it my name you choose to jeopardize
Any you reply, they say you're selfish
Nope, I'm full of self shit
Better than being indulged in someone else
For you can no longer breathe for you are no longer yourself.

Untitled Me

Unbearable and disgruntle am I
Though I feel I have transformed into this creature
Failing to understand and unwilling
Have I lost the battle?
Or have I lost stamina to withstand the beatings
Proclaiming to be structured but realizing I have been broken
Has the recession caused me to recoil?
Fighter I always tell myself, yet I want to give up
Needing others to reassure me
No longer the positive optimist, but negative to all my goals
Trying to help others succeed
Why have I given up the fight?
Fighting with thy inner being
I am being, just not being who I am
But who others see me as unfledged and self-indulged
Though intelligent and determined
I am quirky, unequal, agog, nonchalant, daring, rebellious and ambitious
Not quixotic, unmanly, abrogate, darkling, repugnant, or arid
Better than I before, better I will become
Because I am unlimited only limited by thy self
Me without him but with them
Who are thee, because I have finally found who is me.